BUILD YOUR OWN
SENSATIONAL SPACE PROJECTS

Rob Ives

CONTENTS

PREPARE FOR LIFTOFF	4	SAFETY FIRST!	6

SENSATIONAL SPACE PROJECTS	8	STARRY NIGHT	22
PENDULUM ASTRONAUT	10	ORIGAMI SPACE ROCKET	24
PIPE CLEANER ALIENS	14	COMET CARD	26
PULL-THE-TAB ROCKET	16	LIFE IN SPACE	30
ROBO-DOG	18		

GLOSSARY AND INDEX	32

Copyright © 2024 Hungry Tomato Ltd

First published in 2024 by Hungry Tomato Ltd
F15, Old Bakery Studios, Blewetts Wharf, Malpas Road, Truro, Cornwall,
TR1 1QH, UK.

No part of this publication may be reproduced, stored in a retrieval system, or transmitted in any form or by any means, electronic, mechanical, photocopying, recording, or otherwise, without prior written permission of the copyright owner.
A CIP catalogue record for this book is available from the British Library.

ISBN 9781916598843

Printed in China

Discover more at
www.hungrytomato.com

PREPARE FOR LIFTOFF

Try your hand at building amazing space-themed models! Using smart and simple engineering principles, you can make a whole collection of out-of-this-world crafts that hover, fly, move, and show the wonders of our universe and beyond!

THIS BOOK IS INTERACTIVE!

Some of the projects in this book come with templates to help you cut pieces to the right shape and size. Use a smartphone to scan the QR code at the beginning of the project to access a downloadable template that you can print out.

You will find QR codes at the end of some projects, too. These will direct you to videos of the moving models in action!

You can also find all templates and videos at:
www.hungrytomato.com/space-projects

PREPARE FOR LIFTOFF

TOP TIPS

- Before you start any project, read the step-by-steps all the way through to get an idea of what you are aiming for. The pictures show what the steps tell you.

- When printing templates, check that your printer is set to "print to scale" or to "full size" to make sure they come out the right size for your other materials!

- Use a cutting mat, or similar surface, for cutting lengths of craft sticks, skewers, and anything else you may need.

- Use the sharp end of a pencil to make small holes in cardboard (see page 7 for method) or ask an adult to help, using either scissors or a craft knife.

- Ask an adult to help straighten out and shape paper clips using a pair of pliers.

- Where strong glue is required, you may want to use a glue gun. Make sure you ask permission, and do not use it without an adult present. Strong liquid glue, such as wood or epoxy glue, will work well, too.

You will find stars in the corner of the first page of each craft. These stars are a guide to the difficulty level of each project. They show you when you may need another pair of hands!

SAFETY FIRST!

Be careful and use good sense when making these models. They are easy to understand but will require some cutting, gluing, drilling, and other awkward tasks that you may need some help with from an adult.

WHEN TO GET HELP

Watch out for this sign throughout the book. You may need help from an adult when completing these tasks.

DISCLAIMER

The author, publisher, and bookseller cannot take responsibility for your safety. When you make and try out the projects, you do so at your own risk. Look out for the safety warning symbol (shown left) given throughout the book and call on adult assistance when you are cutting materials or using a pair of scissors or pliers, craft drill, or hot glue.

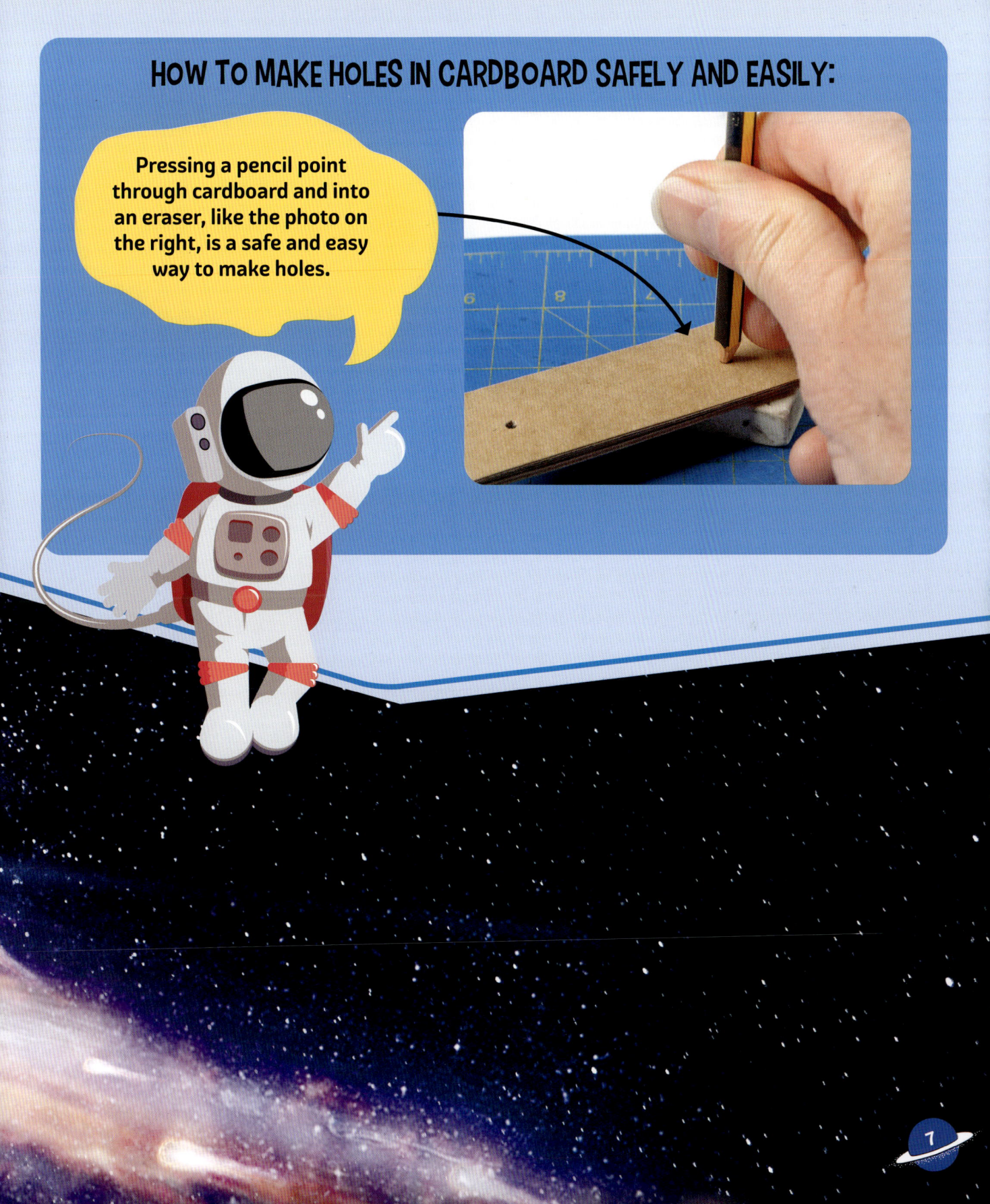

SENSATIONAL SPACE PROJECTS

Outer space is an amazing place that we're learning more about, thanks to scientists making bigger and better machines to explore space with. But we still have lots of questions!

AMAZING ASTRONAUTS
100 years ago, we didn't have the technology to travel into space, but now astronauts exist, and live and work 250 miles above the Earth on the **International Space Station (ISS)**. These brave people make incredible discoveries from space!

SPACE ROBOTS
Scientists are always creating new robots to send to space. They are incredibly helpful for space exploration because they can go to planets that humans can't. We are learning a lot thanks to these fantastic exploring robots!

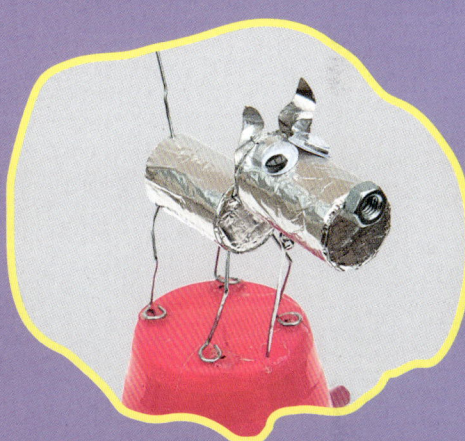

WANT TO KNOW MORE?
This book is full of super space-themed crafts to get your imagination running, as you wonder what it would be like to explore faraway planets and **galaxies...**

PENDULUM ASTRONAUT

Make this amazing astronaut on a pendulum and watch it swing from side to side, as if free-falling through space!

Use the QR code to access the template you need.

WHAT YOU NEED:
- Paper cup
- Bamboo skewer
- Small coins
- Coffee stirrer
- Paper straw
- Stiff black and white card
- Craft stick
- Felt-tip pens or pencils

TOOLS:
- Pencil and eraser
- Ruler
- Pair of scissors
- Strong craft glue
- White paint marker pen

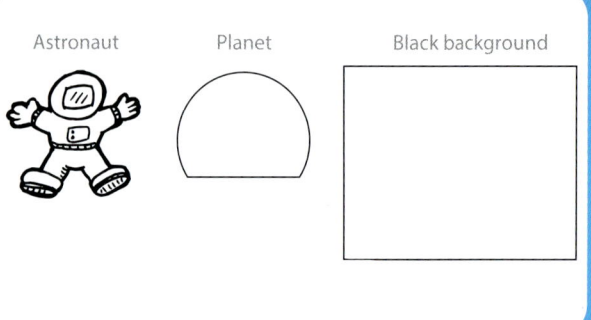

1 Print, copy, or trace the shapes from the template onto the specified materials and cut out. Decorate the planet and astronaut with felt-tip pens or pencils.

2 Turn the paper cup upside down. Measure and cut a length of paper straw so that it's the same length as the bottom of the cup. Set aside until step 5.

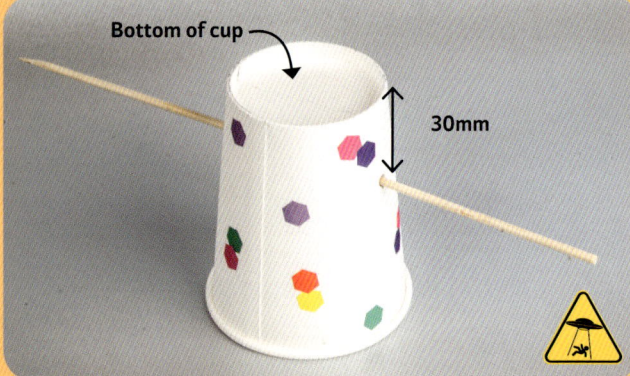

3 Make holes (see page 7) on either side of the cup, 30mm from the bottom. Push skewer through to check the holes line up, then trim so that 12mm remains at each side. Remove the skewer until step 8.

4 Hold the coffee stirrer so that the end touches the lip of the cup. Use a pencil to mark the stirrer where it lines up with the hole in the cup.

DID YOU KNOW?
It can take up to 2 years of intense training to become a fully qualified astronaut. Don't worry; this astronaut won't take as long to make!

5 Glue the straw to the stirrer where you marked it in step 4, in the position shown above.

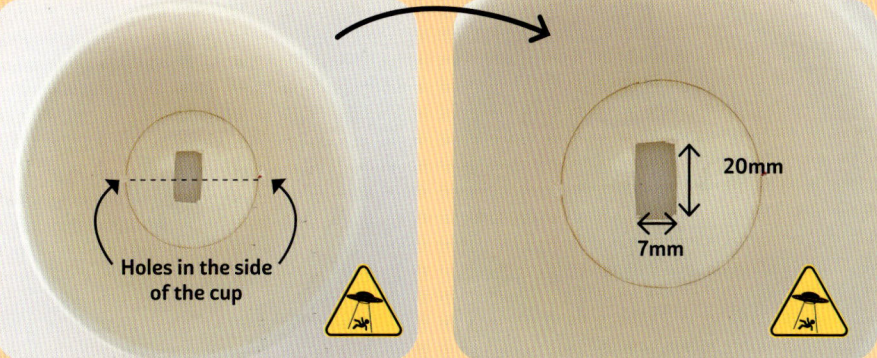

6 Glue a coin to each side of the stirrer on the end that had been on the lip of the cup.

7 Ask an adult to help you cut a 7mm x 20mm rectangle out of the bottom of the cup. The middle of the long side of the rectangle should line up with the holes you made in the side of the cup.

8 Thread the stirrer and straw up into the cup, with the coins pointing toward the lip of the cup. Line the straw up with the holes and thread the skewer through to hold it in place.

9 Glue the skewers into place. The stirrer should still be free to swing back and forth like a pendulum.

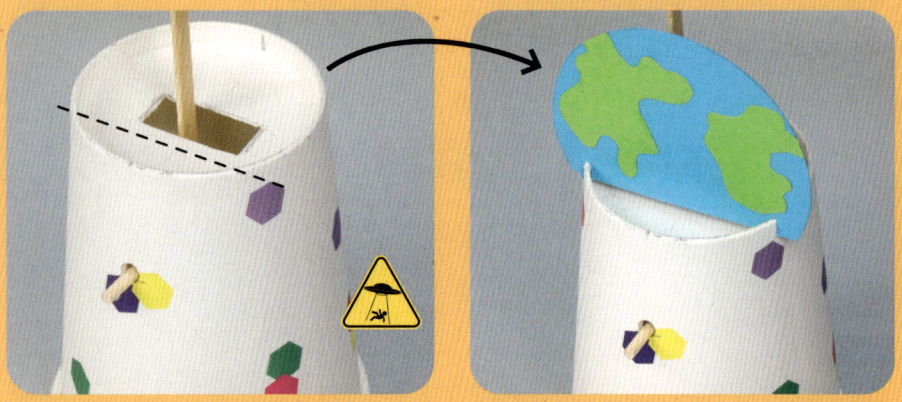 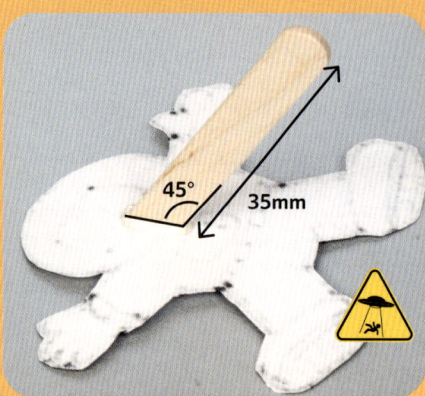

10 Make two small cuts near the front of the cup. They should be parallel with the long side of the rectangular hole and halfway between this and the front of the cup as shown. Then, fit your planet in. It shouldn't touch the stirrer.

11 Cut a craft stick to a length of 35mm. Glue the angled end to the back of the astronaut from the template as shown.

 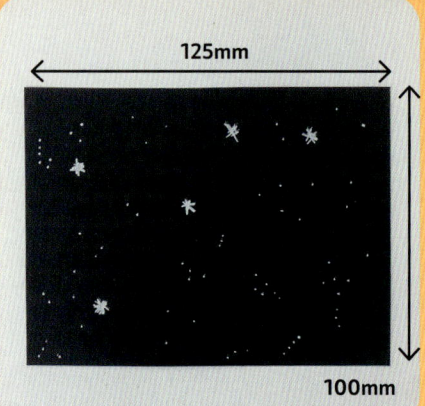 

12 Glue the astronaut's craft stick to the pendulum stirrer so it can swing without touching the planet as shown.

13 Cut a piece of stiff black card to 125 x 100mm. Create a **star field** with a white paint marker.

14 Make two small cuts near the back of the cup, behind the pendulum. Fit the black card in, making sure everything remains free to move.

DID YOU KNOW?
Astronauts sometimes complete **spacewalks**. This means they get out of their spacecraft while in space! They do this to carry out experiments, or repair **satellites** or spacecraft.

TOP TIP

Decorate your cup and astronaut however you like!

TAP THE ASTRONAUT TO SET THE PENDULUM SWINGING FROM SIDE TO SIDE!

PIPE CLEANER ALIENS

Making glittery aliens is a fun project to stretch your imagination. Here are a few examples you can try to get you going!

WHAT YOU NEED:
- Assorted tinsel pipe cleaners
- Corrugated cardboard
- Pom poms (assorted sizes)
- Plastic eyes

TOOLS:
- Pencil/pen (for curling the pipe cleaners)
- Pair of scissors
- Strong craft glue

1 Cut out a small circle of corrugated cardboard, 50mm in diameter.

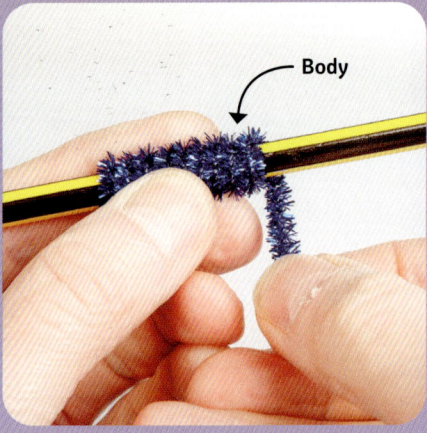

2 Wrap a tinsel pipe cleaner around a pencil, then slide it off. This will be the body.

3 Use strong glue to stick the alien's body to the middle of the cardboard circle.

4 Wrap a pipe cleaner once around the body, horizontally, leaving the two ends sticking out like arms as shown.

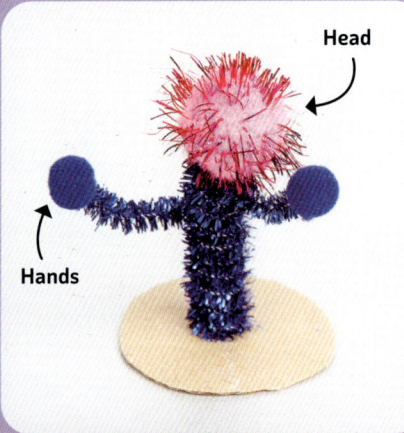

5 Glue on small pom poms to make the alien's hands. Glue on a larger pom pom to make the alien's head.

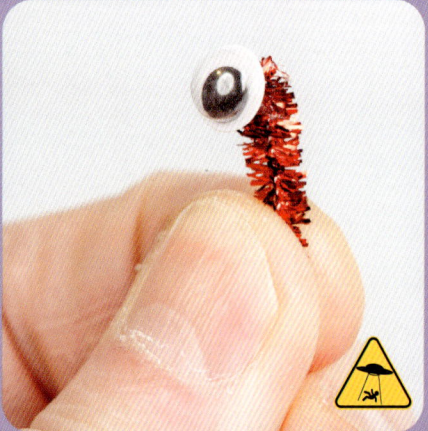

6 Make an eye stalk with another pipe cleaner, cutting it to a shorter size if you like. Glue a plastic eye to the end. Repeat to make a second.

7 Glue the eye stalks to the alien's head to complete the first alien.

TOP TIP
Try making other designs with different numbers of eyes, heads, and arms! How strange can you make them look?

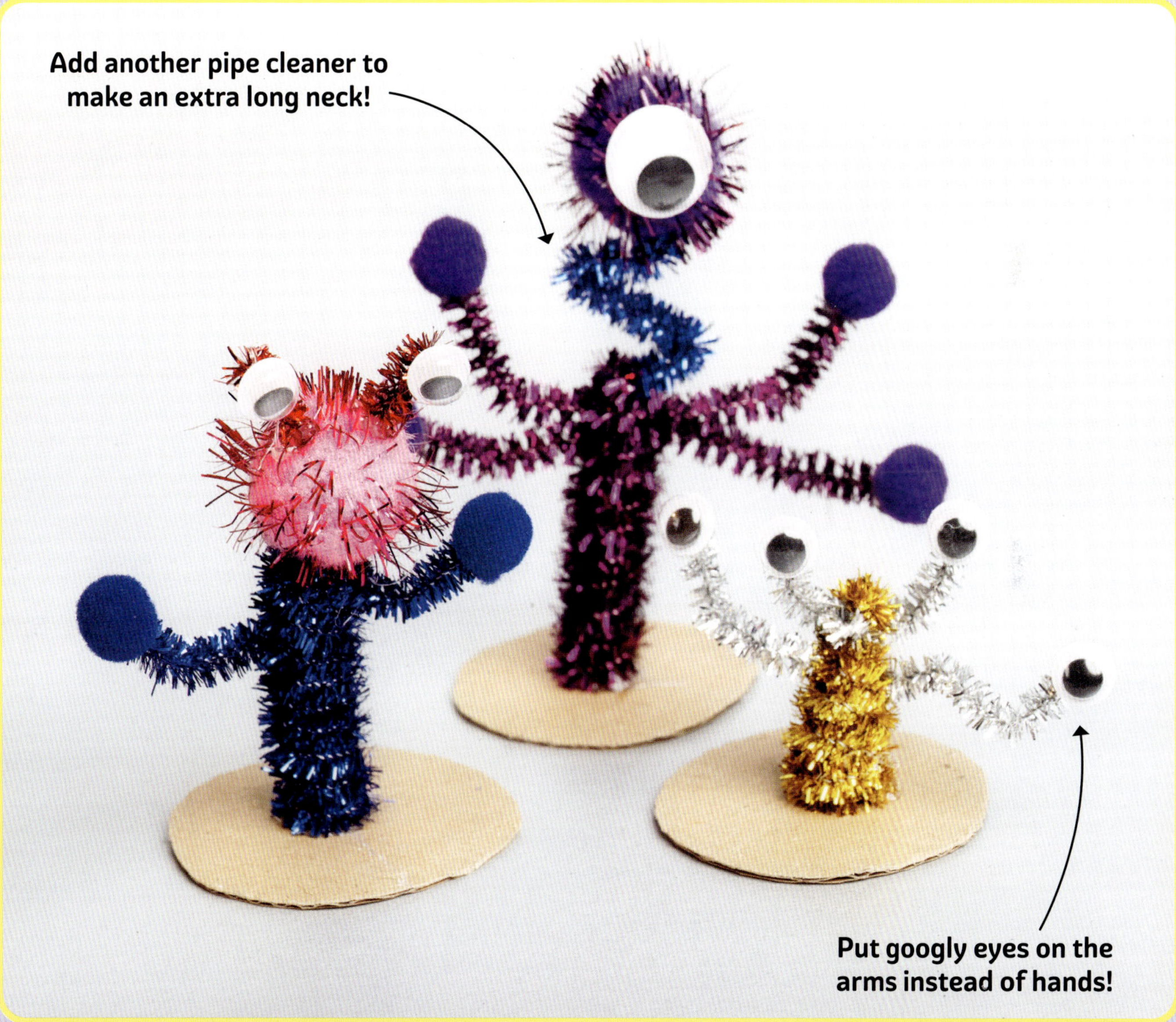

Add another pipe cleaner to make an extra long neck!

Put googly eyes on the arms instead of hands!

LET YOUR IMAGINATION RUN WILD AS YOU MAKE YOUR OWN DESIGNS!

PULL-THE-TAB ROCKET

Blast into outer space with this spectacular pull-the-tab rocket craft!

Use the QR code to access the template you need.

WHAT YOU NEED:
- Assorted card
- Felt-tip pens or pencils

TOOLS:
- Pair of scissors
- Strong craft glue

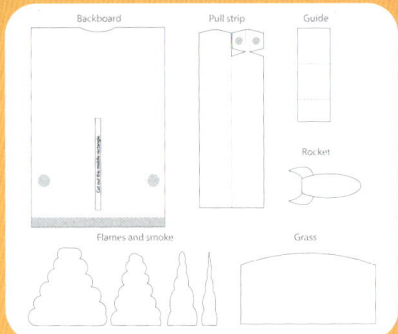

1 Print, copy, or trace the shapes from the template onto the specified materials and cut out.

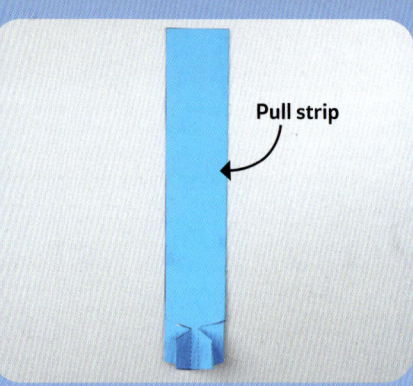

2 Fold the pull strip along the dotted lines indicated on the template and glue down all folds except for the tabs – leave them raised up as shown.

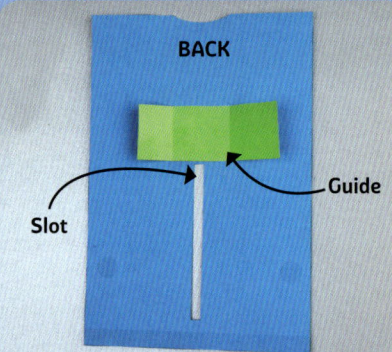

3 Turn the back board so that the back is facing you. Glue the guide to the back board above the slot.

4 Thread the tabs from the pull strip into the slot in the back board.

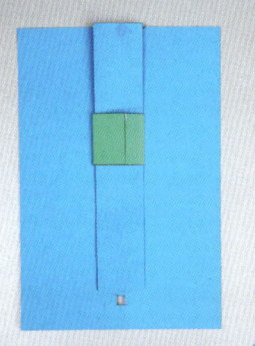

5 Glue the guide over the pull strip so that it can still move up and down.

6 Glue together the layers of flame and smoke in size order as shown.

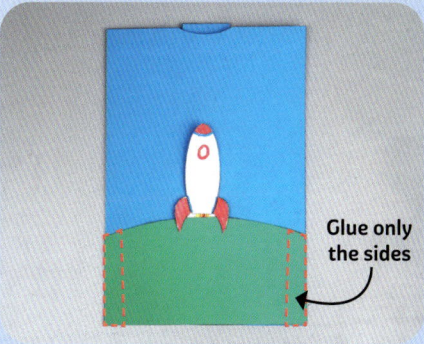

7 Flip the back board over, then place the flames over the middle of the slot. Glue the furthest edges to the back board.

8 Decorate your rocket with felt-tip pens and pencils. Then, glue it to the top of the flames.

9 Cover the lower part of the flames with the grass, gluing it to the back board at each side, where indicated above.

Glue only the sides

PULL THE TAB TO LAUNCH THE ROCKET!

ROBO-DOG

Robo-dog is the perfect companion for space travel. Would you explore faraway planets and galaxies with this four-legged friend?

WHAT YOU NEED:
- 2 small craft corks
- Tin foil
- Plastic cup
- Small metal nut
- Corrugated cardboard
- Jumbo paper clips
- Plastic eyes

TOOLS:
- Ruler
- Needle pliers
- Wire cutters
- Strong craft glue
- Craft drill
- Pencil and eraser
- Sticky tape

1 Take the two corks and cover with tin foil. Secure in place with craft glue.

2 Ask an adult to straighten out a jumbo paper clip and push it through the cork about 75mm from one end.

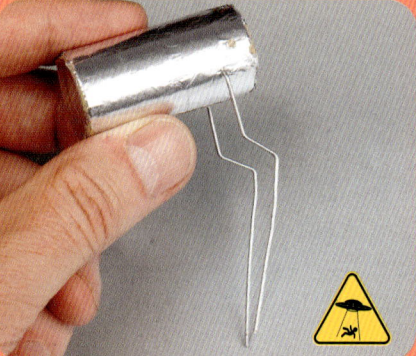

3 Use pliers to shape the wire downward to make rear legs.

4 Fold the wire around to make knees and paws. Snip off any excess wire.

5 Repeat steps 2-4 at the front of the cork to make front legs.

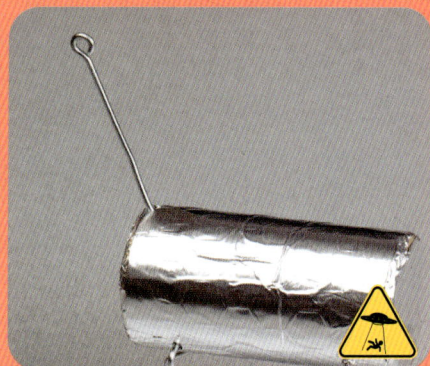

6 Add a small loop to a straightened out paper clip to make a tail. Set aside the body until step 9.

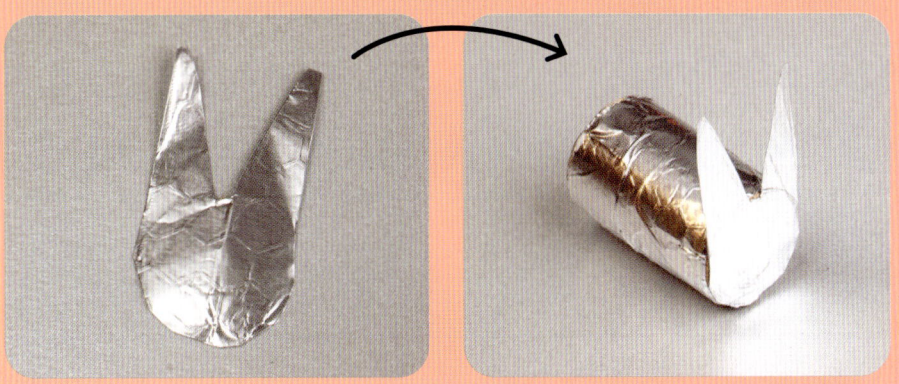

7 Use a double thickness of foil to make the dog ears. Then, glue the ears to the back of the second cork.

8 Turn the cork so that the ears are at the back, then fold them forward a little to make them more realistic.

FOLLOW THESE STEPS TO MAKE IT STAND!

Follow step 9 below if you want to make a mini standing Robo-dog model. Skip straight to step 10 (on page 20) if you want to make it move instead!

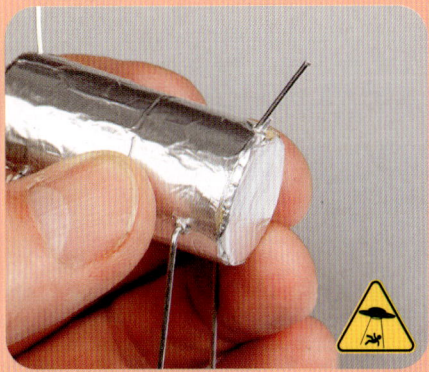

9 Add a short length of wire from a paper clip to the front of the body to make a neck.

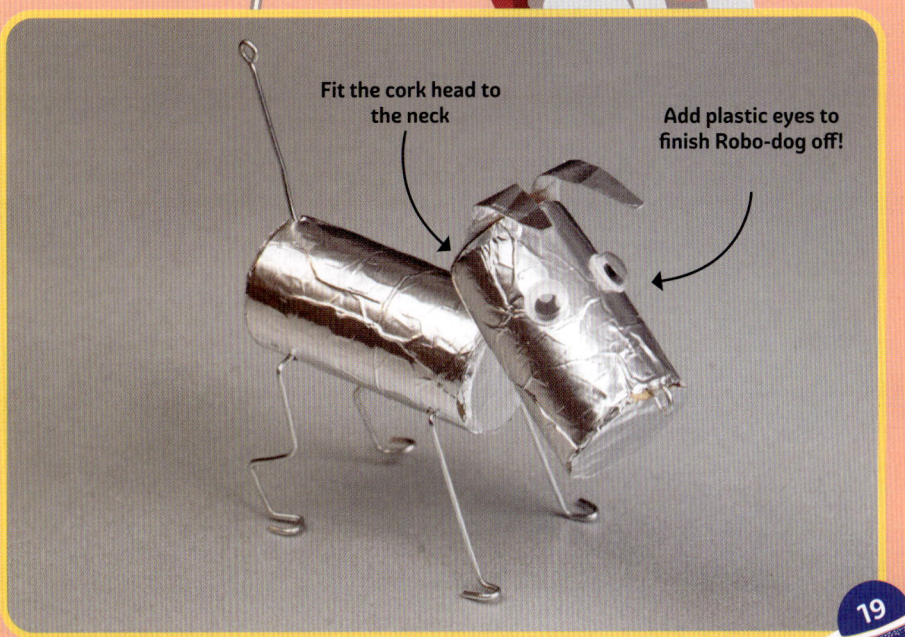

Fit the cork head to the neck

Add plastic eyes to finish Robo-dog off!

FOLLOW THESE STEPS TO MAKE IT MOVE!

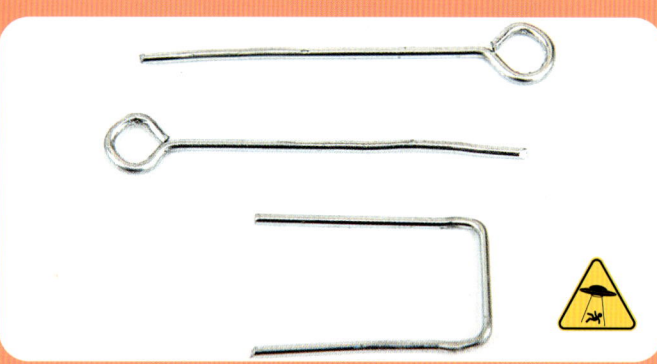

10 Ask an adult to make these wire pieces from an unfolded paper clip using pliers.

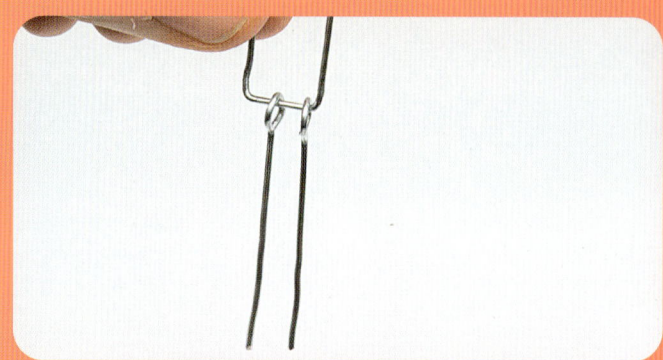

11 Thread the loops into the "U" shape to make into the neck staple.

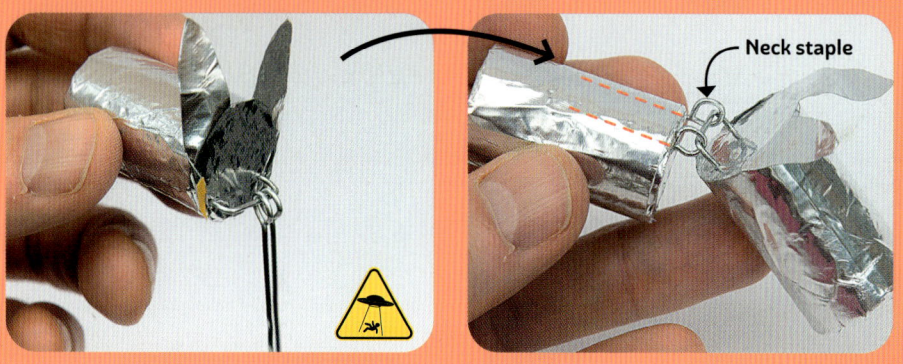

12 Push the ends of the neck staple into the lower part of the head, and fit the other ends of the loop pieces to the top of the body so that the head is free to move up and down.

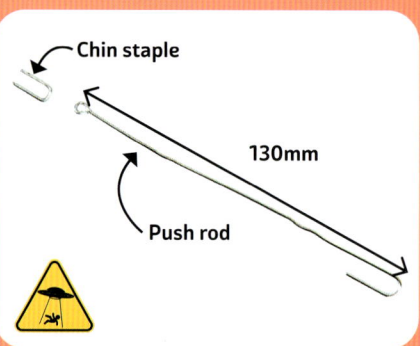

13 Unfold another paper clip and make the push rod pieces as shown. Cut off a 50mm piece for the chin staple.

14 Hook the push rod over the chin staple. Push the chin staple into the dog's chin. Set Robo-dog aside until step 18.

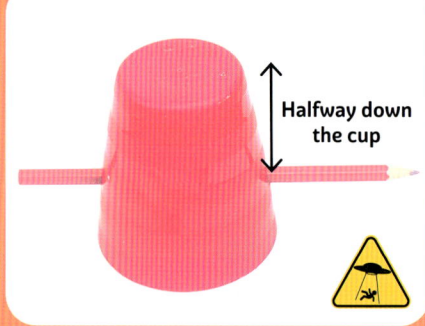

15 Drill holes in opposite sides of the cup, halfway down. Make them big enough for the pencil to fit through.

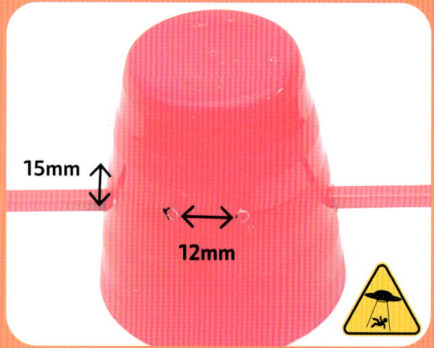

16 Drill two smaller holes in between the pencil holes. They should be 15mm above these and 12mm apart.

Staple

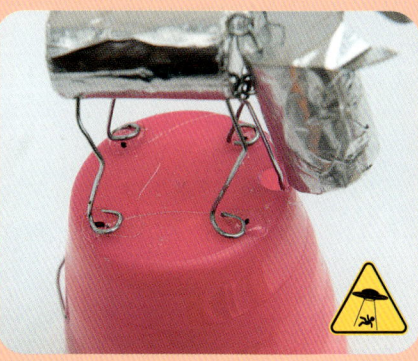

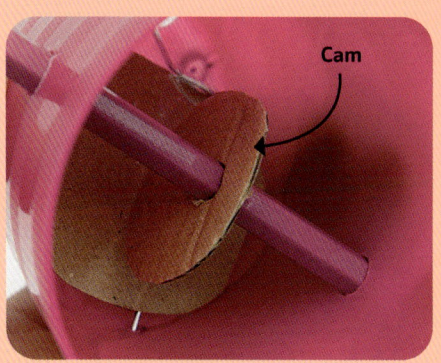
Cam

17 Cut out a rough cardboard circle. Use a paper clip to make a staple for the cup. Push it through the small holes in the cup. Then, push it through the cardboard as shown.

18 Place Robo-dog on the upside-down cup, mark where its feet are and drill a hole between the front feet. Thread the push rod through, then glue each foot down in place.

19 Tape the push rod to the cardboard circle. Make a cam from a 30mm circle of cardboard, with a hole in the middle (see page 7).

Cardboard washer

20 Thread the pencil into the cup and cam as shown. Cut the pencil so that 20mm remains at each side of the cup.

21 Make a 25mm cardboard washer. Add it to the left end of the pencil as Robo-dog faces you.

22 Straighten a paper clip and wrap one end around the right end of the pencil. Shape the rest into a handle.

Add plastic eyes and a nose to finish Robo-dog off!

TWIST THE HANDLE TO MAKE ROBO-DOG MOVE!

STARRY NIGHT

TOP TIP

If you don't have a paintbrush, you could use a glue spreader/spatula, sponges, or even your fingers!

Let's make an impressionist print based loosely on the famous painting 'Starry Night' by Van Gogh. Take a peek at the real deal on page 23 for inspiration before you start!

WHAT YOU NEED:
- Cutting board – larger than your piece of paper
- Assorted plain paper
- Tin foil
- Sticky tape
- Poster paints

TOOLS:
- Pair of scissors
- Wooden stirrers
- Paintbrush

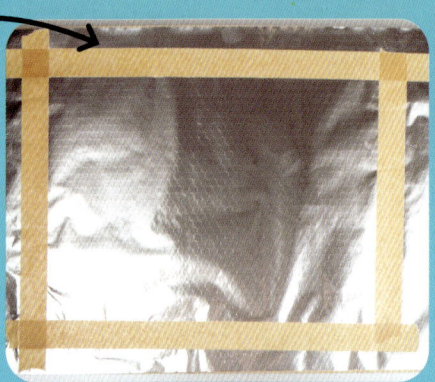

1 Cover one side of the cutting board with tin foil. Then, place the paper you want to print onto in the middle of the foil. Stick tape around the edges, but be careful it doesn't touch or hold the paper down. Lift the paper away to reveal a frame for your print area.

2 Scoop out the paints using a wooden stirrer and use the edge of the foil outside the print area as a mixing area.

3 Make expressive swirls of paint to fill the foil. Mix blue paint with black or white to change how dark the sky is.

4 Use yellow paint to make stars on the foil. Swirl the paints together to mix them into an explosion of shades and patterns.

5 Once happy with your design, carefully place your paper over the print area. Try not to let it slide side to side as you do so.

6 Press down over the whole area to transfer the paint to the paper.

7 Start in one corner and carefully peel the paper off the foil to reveal your masterpiece!

TOP TIP

To clean your paintbrush between using different paints, swish in a paper cup filled with plain water, and dry on a paper towel.

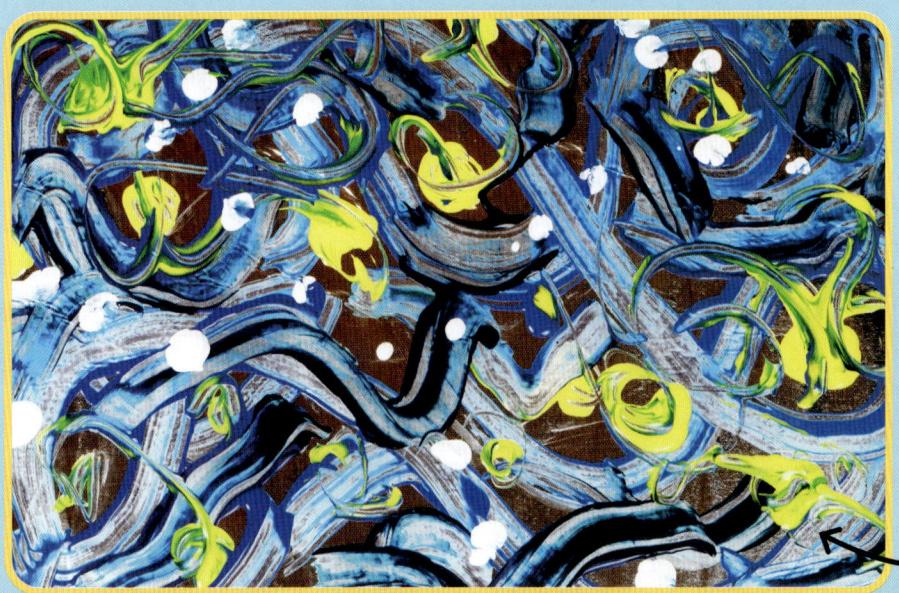

BE CREATIVE! EXPERIMENT WITH DIFFERENT PAPER, TOOLS AND PAINTS!

'Starry Night' by Van Gogh

ORIGAMI SPACE ROCKET

TOP TIP

Origami is a lot easier to follow when watching a video! Scan the QR code to watch how to make it.

This rocket is similar to the ones that were used to transport things to the International Space Station.

Use the QR code to see a video of the steps in action.

WHAT YOU NEED:
- Origami paper 150 x 150mm square

1 Start with a single square sheet of paper with the diagonals, vertical and horizontal lines creased.

2 Fold from the top right corner to the bottom left. Then, tuck in the other two corners to make a smaller square. Rotate the square 45 degrees so that the open end is at the bottom.

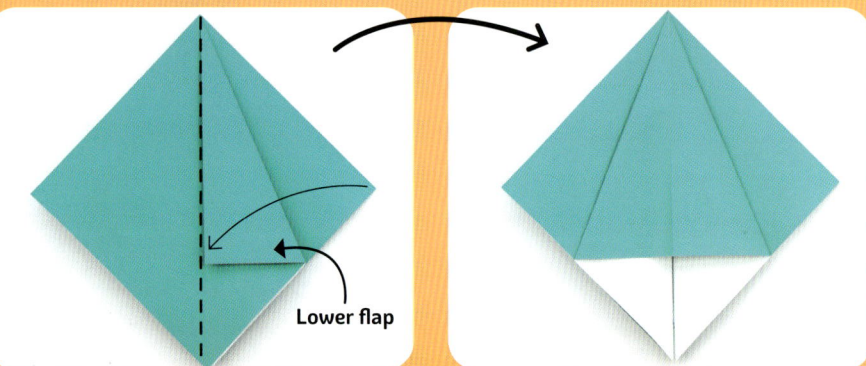

3 Fold in the right corner to the middle line to create a crease. Pull the lower flap out from underneath (by inserting your fingers under the folded area). Open out and flatten the fold by pulling the flap to the bottom left edge to make an inverted kite shape. Crease the paper in place.

4 Flip the paper over and repeat step 3 three more times with the other flaps, until it looks like the image above.

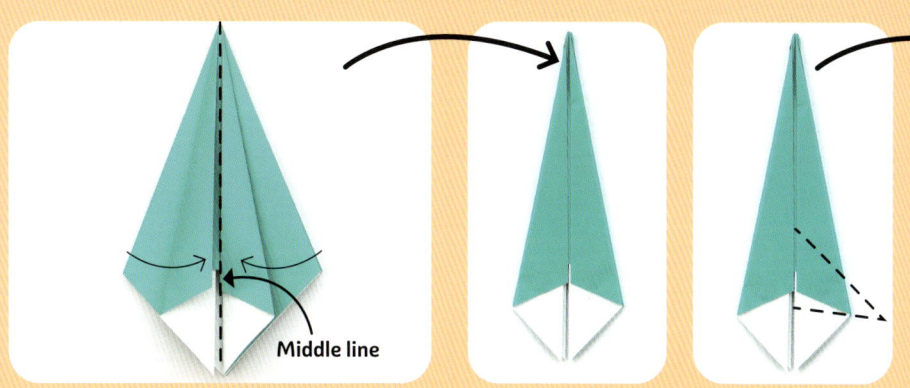
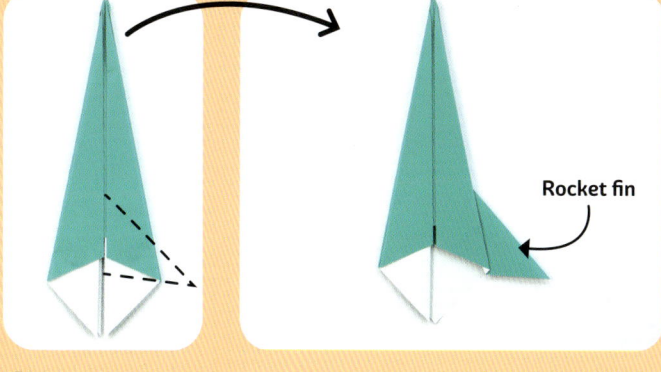

5 Fold the outer left and right corners to the vertical middle line and crease along the fold. Flip the paper over and repeat three more times with the other flaps.

6 Lift up the bottom flap, fold it in on itself, and pull the foot out to make a rocket fin.

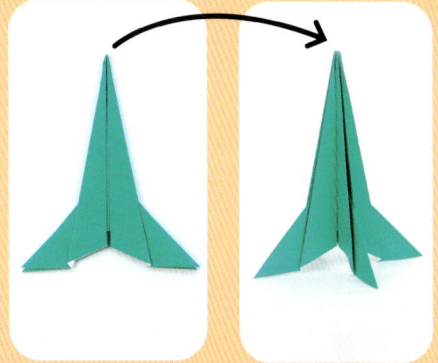

7 Repeat step 6 with the other three fins. Then, open out the model to complete the rocket.

Sharp and neat folding is important to make the final model look great!

DID YOU KNOW?
The first rocket-like objects that could fly were small fireworks. It took humans centuries to build rockets capable of flying into outer space!

COMET CARD

Impress your friends and family with this amazing moving card. Open and close it to watch the **comet** soar over the Earth!

Use the QR code to access the template you need.

WHAT YOU NEED:
- Assorted card
- 2 pieces of stiff black card
- White paint marker pen
- Felt-tip pens or pencils

TOOLS:
- Ruler
- Pair of scissors
- Strong craft glue

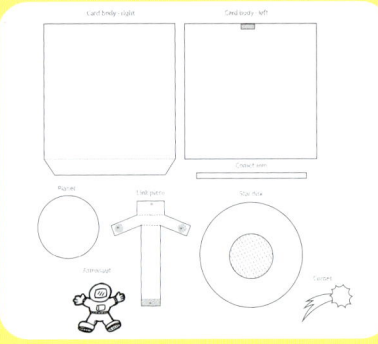

1 Print, copy, or trace the shapes from the templates onto the specified materials and cut out.

2 Decorate the comet and planet with felt-tip pens, pencils, or different bits of card.

3 Use a white paint marker pen to add a starry field background to the ring.

4 Glue the two black card squares from the template together to make one large card. Fold along the middle crease, then open out again.

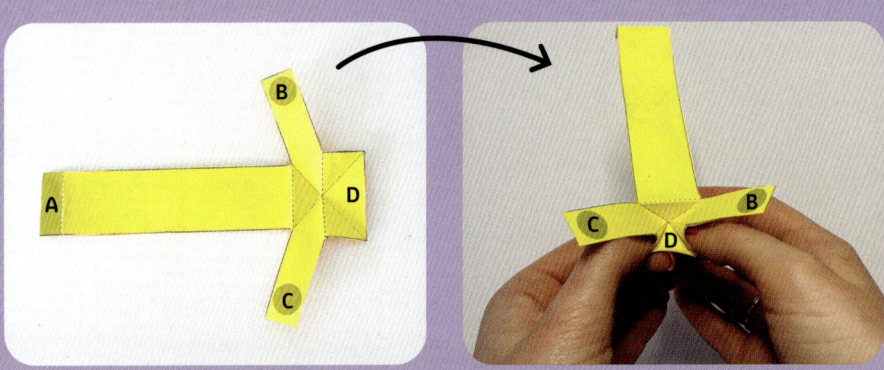

5 Take the link piece and fold along the lines indicated on the template to create creases. Use the images above to see how to fold the link piece correctly. Our link pieces are bright colours to make it visually easier for you to follow, but you should use black card for the best effect.

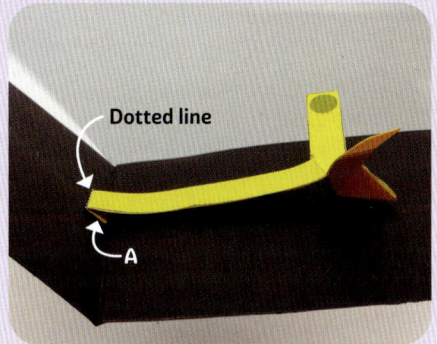
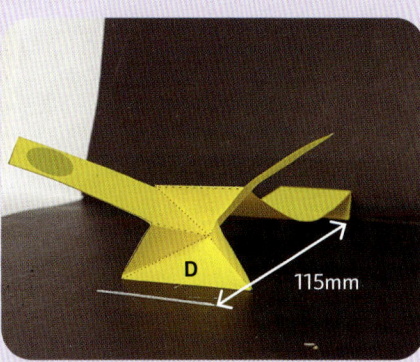

Make sure section C is in front of the ring

6 Fold section A on the link piece along the dotted line. Add glue to section A, then stick the flap to the inside cover as shown.

7 Mark a line 115mm from the card crease. Add glue to the back of section D, pull it to the line and press down.

8 Add glue to the tip of section B on the link piece. Thread the ring into the position shown to stick the ring to section B.

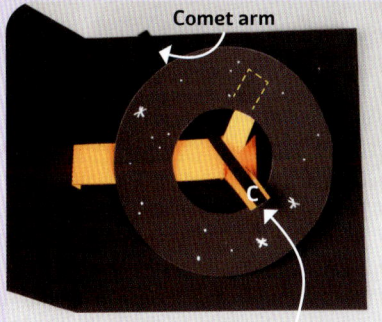

Glue the comet arm to section C

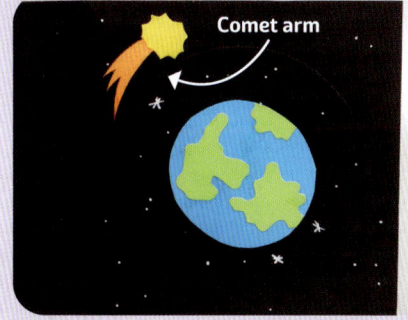

9 Thread the comet arm through the ring hole. Line it up with section C and glue the tips of each together as shown.

10 Place the planet over the ring so that it's directly over the middle of the hole, then glue the back of the planet to section C.

11 Glue your comet to the top of the comet arm. Then, add a few more stars to the background to complete your card.

12 Decorate the front of your card to finish it off! Use the astronaut template or draw your own design.

DID YOU KNOW?
Scientists name comets, usually after the person or spacecraft that discovered them. They've discovered thousands of different comets!

27

DID YOU KNOW?
Comets are giant snowballs made of frozen gas, rock, and dust. As they get close to the Sun, they heat up. This makes it looks like they're glowing and creates the long tail they're known for.

OPEN AND CLOSE YOUR CARD TO SEE THE COMET FLY OVER EARTH!

LIFE IN SPACE

The International Space Station (ISS) is the largest human-made object ever put into space. Astronauts from 15 different countries spend months on board, carrying out different experiments. So, what is it like to live in outer space?

GOODBYE GRAVITY

Living in outer space means saying farewell to **gravity**! Astronauts are constantly floating around - how strange must that feel? There are many everyday things that are different in outer space.

SURVIVING SPACE

Food is carefully prepared to avoid spoiling and astronauts can only drink from pouches through a straw, as liquids in a cup would float out! They can't wash like we do on Earth so use "rinseless" shampoo to clean their hair. It would have taken a long time to figure this all out!

SPACE PROJECTS

There are many cool experiments happening on the ISS, such as studying how plants grow without gravity and how our bodies work in space. These projects help astronauts learn how humans can live in space for longer amounts of time!

SURVIVING SPACE

The ISS is designed to make sure astronauts have everything they need while in space. There are machines that make sure there's enough **oxygen**, as well as systems that clean the air, so it stays fresh. The ISS also has strong walls to protect astronauts from harmful space rays and the Sun.

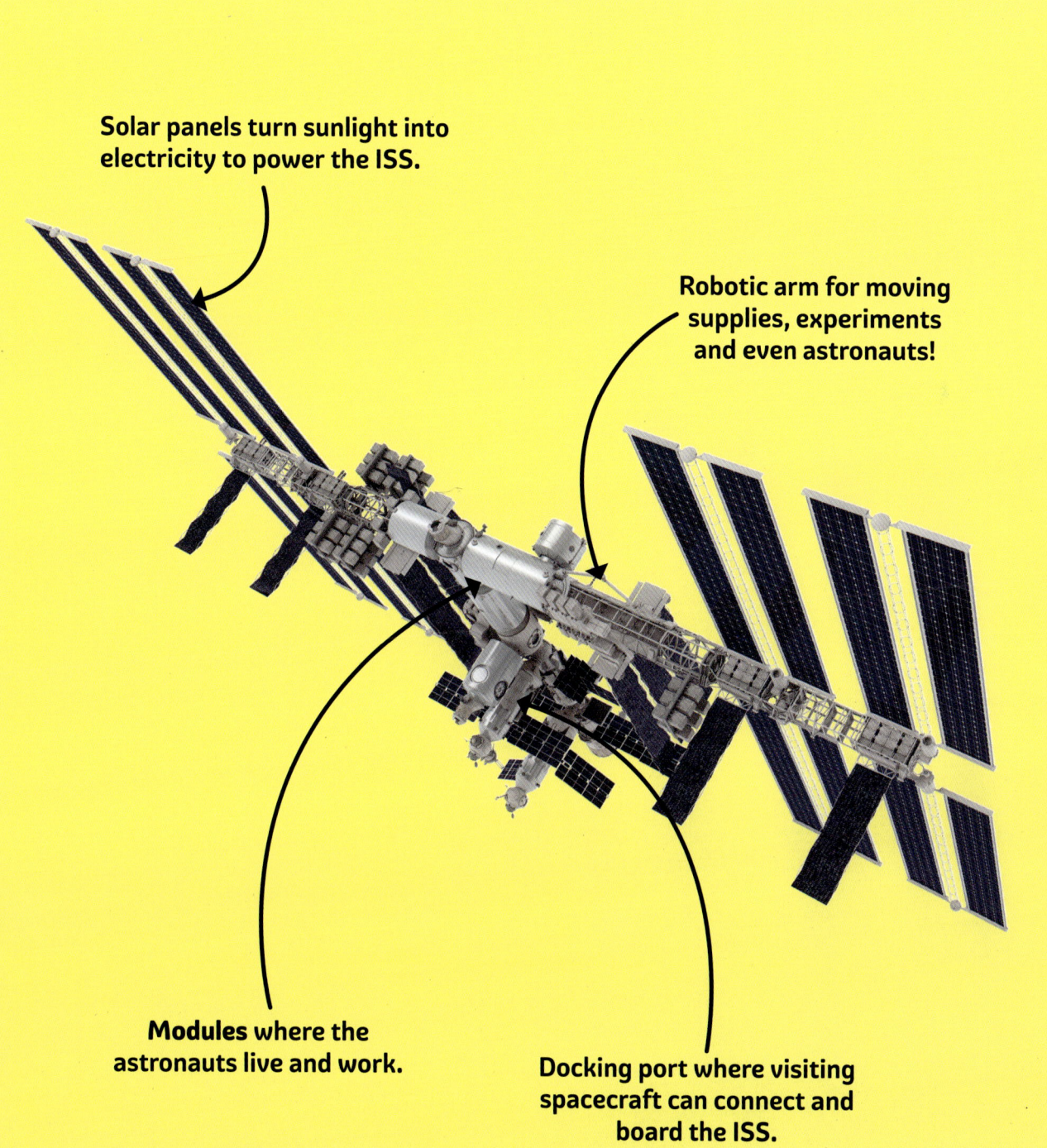

Solar panels turn sunlight into electricity to power the ISS.

Robotic arm for moving supplies, experiments and even astronauts!

Modules where the astronauts live and work.

Docking port where visiting spacecraft can connect and board the ISS.

GLOSSARY

Comet - a large flying space object that's made of frozen gas, rock, and dust. As they get closer to the Sun, they heat up and appear to leave a glowing streak behind them.

Galaxy – a huge collection of gas, dust, and billions of stars and their solar systems, all held together by gravity (see right).

Gravity - a pulling force that works across space. Objects don't have to touch each other for gravity to affect them. For example, the Sun, which is millions of miles away, pulls on Earth and the other planets and objects in the solar system to keep them in orbit.

International Space Station (ISS) - a large spacecraft that orbits the Earth, where astronauts live and work.

Modules - self-contained sections of a spacecraft. The ISS (see above) is made up of lots of different modules.

Oxygen - an invisible gas in the air that people and animals need to breathe.

Satellites - machines in space that work as cameras and messengers, helping humans in many ways.

Spacewalks - when astronauts leave their spacecraft and float around in space.

Star field - a group of stars visible to the human eye.

INDEX

A
aliens 14-15
astronauts 9, 10-11, 12-13, 27, 30-31

C
comets 26-27, 28-29

E
Earth 9, 26, 30
experiments 12, 23, 30-31

G
gravity 30, 32

I
International Space Station (ISS) 9, 30, 31, 32

P
pendulum 10-11, 12-13

R
robots 9, 18-19, 20-21, 31
rockets 16-17, 24-25

S
satellite 12, 32
spacewalk 12, 32
stars 12, 22-23, 26
Sun 28, 31

PICTURE CREDITS:

(Abbreviations: t=top, b=bottom, m=middle, l=left, r=right, bg=background)

Shutterstock: Andrei Armiagov 30tr; Creativeshoot IDN 30ml; Dima Zel 31m; FishCoolish Astronaut character throughout; Klyaksun spaceship/rocket throughout; Marko Aliaksandr 29bg; NASA Images 8b, 2-3b; Spatuletail 23b.

Every effort has been made to trace the copyright holders, and we apologise in advance for any unintentional omissions. We would be pleased to insert the appropriate acknowledgements in any subsequent edition of this publication.

BUILD YOUR OWN SENSATIONAL SPACE PROJECTS

Build your own out-of-this-world space-themed models! Using recycled materials and easy-to-find craft supplies, you can make a whole collection of spectacular space projects, including:

- **AWESOME ROCKETS READY FOR LIFTOFF**
- **A SUPER SPACEWALKING ASTRONAUT**
- **AMAZING ALIENS FROM DISTANT GALAXIES**

And much more! Test your engineering and model-making skills, and discover more about our incredible solar system and beyond.

Robo-dog

Pipe cleaner aliens

Check out all of the books in the **'Build Your Own Space Projects'** series by Rob Ives:

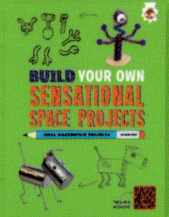
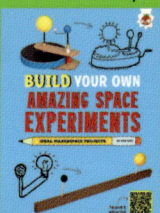

www.hungrytomato.com

ISBN 978-1-916598-84-3

9 781916 598843

RRP £9.99